Eve in Exile
Group Discussion
Study Guide

Published by Canon Press
P.O. Box 8729, Moscow, Idaho 83843
800.488.2034 | www.canonpress.com

Canon Press, *Eve in Exile Group Discussion Study Guide*
Copyright ©2022 by Canon Press.

Cover design by James Engerbretson
Interior design by Valerie Anne Bost

Printed in the United States of America.

All rights reserved. No part of this publication may be reproduced, stored in a retrieval system, or transmitted in any form by any means, electronic, mechanical, photocopy, recording, or otherwise, without prior permission of the author, except as provided by USA copyright law.

Library of Congress Cataloging-in-Publication Data

Eve in exile : group discussion study guide.
Moscow, Idaho : Canon Press, [2022]
LCCN 2022005074 | ISBN 9781954887466 (paperback)
LCSH: Merkle, Rebekah. Eve in exile. | Women—Religious aspects—Christianity—Textbooks. | Femininity—Religious aspects—Christianity—Textbooks.
Classification: LCC BT704.M5453 E94 2022 | DDC 248.8/43—dc23/eng/20220412
LC record available at https://lccn.loc.gov/2022005074

INTRODUCTION:
THE FREEDOM OF LIMITS

Summary:
Our culture has torn down the old version of femininity, but has nothing to offer in its place. It's time to rebuild.

Highlights:
"We have a fantastic opportunity in front of us, but we also have a hostile audience. We are in the position of Nehemiah–returning from exile and trying to rebuild the walls of Jerusalem while the culture outside jeers. But

if I could stand in any moment, this is the one I would pick. We have a huge opportunity in front of us, and I hope we can make the most of it. The way of return is open to us—but it will require strong women who are willing to show actual courage if we truly want to bring Eve back from exile." (12-13)

Questions for Discussion and Application:
1. Why does Bekah Merkle describe "limits" as "freeing"?

2. What is the great opportunity Christians face in this cultural moment?

3. What did your parents teach you growing up about what it means to be a woman? What has the church taught you about gender roles? Has your experience been prairie-muffins or pant-suits—or something in between these two extremes?

Study the Word:
Read Nehemiah 4 and 6. How does Nehemiah respond to the threats of his enemies? How does he deal with them when they try to lure him into a trap? What are some typical ways the

media attacks Christians today? How do unbelievers shame or manipulate Christians to try to make them compromise?

1
PRETENDYVILLE

Summary:
We cannot retreat into the past.

Highlights:
"A little bit of research into Regency England would show us that, despite the fact that the dresses may have been cute, the society was actually horrifically corrupt. Yes, the BBC 'Pride and Prejudice' series just seems so wholesome and proper and upstanding that it may be hard

to believe, but if you just take a moment to research the life of Lord Byron, a flagrantly immoral, bisexual, incestuous, and nonetheless greatly admired celebrity during Jane Austen's life, or the goings-ons of the Prince Regent and his compadres during the time that she was writing her books, you would very soon discover that the Kardashians have nothing on these people." (23)

"God hasn't called us to run away from the world.... Paul expects the Christians to live in such a way that there is a marked difference between their lifestyle and that of the surrounding unbelievers, but he certainly assumes that they would be in living distinctively in the midst of surrounding ungodliness. He doesn't want us to run away from the world; he actually expects us to charge at the world. To change the world." (24)

Questions for Discussion and Application:
1. What is the problem with conservative-Christian nostalgia for previous eras' gender roles? Why does Bekah call this nostalgia escapist?

2. What is the dominion mandate? What is the great commission? Why is understanding these concepts necessary for understanding femininity?

Study the Word:
Read Ecclesiastes 1:1-11, 2:12-16, and 7:10. Why are people often tempted to say that older times were better? Is there anything really new under the sun?

2

THE MYTHICAL FOUNDATION OF FULFILLMENT

Summary:
Our culture constantly preaches that women should achieve their full potential through their careers instead of serving as mothers and wives.

Highlights:

"Your personal hopes, desires, or opportunities trump all else, and sacrificing your dreams for someone else is not seen as noble, it's seen as ludicrous. If you lay down your 'life' for another, you certainly won't get respect or admiration from our society, and you will definitely get disdain. By many, your choice will just be seen as downright offensive. This overwhelming cultural peer pressure can be a large part of what dupes many women into accepting abortion as a solution to 'a problem.' Promised a quick fix, the sad reality is that these women can often suffer from the emotional damage of their choice for the rest of their lives." (31-32)

"God loves to use the seemingly trivial things to accomplish staggering results. We may each feel like an insignificant little drop of water, and it may seem like the direction we take in our day-to-day lives doesn't make any difference to anyone. But when all the drops of water move the same way, what is more powerful and unstoppable than a wave?" (36)

Questions for Discussion and Application:
1. Why do people think that women have settled when they become wives or homemakers? What do people think it looks like for a woman to be fulfilled?

2. How does the culture's vision of the fulfilled life fall short of the Biblical ideal? How does it compare to Christ's promise that those who lose their life will save it?

3. Why does our culture repeat the lie of fulfillment so often? How do we try to convince ourselves that it is true?

Study the Word:
Read Luke 22:24-27 and John 13:1-17. Who does Jesus say the disciples are not to be like? Why do you think Jesus dealt with this temptation in his disciples so much? How does this command apply to both men and women?

3

PROTO-FEMINISM

Summary:
Feminism began in Europe with Enlightenment thinkers experimenting with egalitarianism and free love.

Highlights:
"A woman raising her children is not only shaping the next generation, she is also shaping little humans who are going to live forever. The souls she gave birth to are immortal. Immortal.

And somehow, our culture looks at a woman who treats that as if it might be an important task and says, 'It's a shame she's wasting herself. She could be doing something important—like filing paperwork for insurance claims.' How did we get to this point?" (42)

"Feminism did not spring up, armed and dangerous, in the 1960s when Gloria Steinem started making headlines—actually, by the time that abortion was legalized in America, feminism was close on two hundred years old. This is important because far too often conservatives want to reject the unsavory fruits of feminism without ever pausing to wonder about the orchard where the fruit was cultivated. They are like dissatisfied movie watchers who, offended by the distasteful final scene in the film, want to rewind it five minutes and then try again, hoping for a different outcome 'this time.'" (42-43)

Questions for Discussion and Application:
1. Why do even conservative Christian housewives feel the need to prove that they are not stupid?

2. What was proto-feminism? What did William Godwin and Mary Wollstonecraft believe? How did their child, Mary Shelley, live out what they taught?

Study the Word:
Read Matthew 10:32-39 and 1 Corinthians 1:18-31. Is following Jesus going to be popular most of the time? Why is it that people who are socially at the bottom are often open to the Gospel? How do respectability and social pressures affect how you think about gender roles?

4
FIRST-WAVE FEMINISM

Summary:
In America, First-Wave Feminism began with women campaigning for votes and birth control.

Highlights:
"Is being childless a bigger advantage to a woman than being gifted, smart, or educated? Are children the bushel under which women are forced to hide their light? Apparently so.

If women wanted to pursue successful, intellectual careers, they needed to not have children . . . and this meant they needed to remain married to their work, maintain a celibate existence, and have nothing to do with men. Nuns renounce sex to become 'married to Christ'; the early feminists had to renounce sex in order to be wed to their careers." (51)

Questions for Discussion and Application:
1. Who were Elizabeth Cady Stanton and Susan B. Anthony? What made Susan B. Anthony so much more famous than Stanton? How was their feminism different from the feminism of Wollstonecraft?

2. What did Sanger advocate that was different from Anthony? Why was birth control so important for feminism? What was eugenics?

Study the Word:
Read 1 Kings 11. How did Solomon's sin begin? Was it obvious to everyone at first? How did Solomon set Israel and Judah on a bad trajectory for the next few hundred years, despite the fact that he was mostly a good king?

5

PSYCHOTROPICS AND SECOND-WAVE FEMINISM

Summary:

Second-Wave Feminism was dissatisfied with the meager role allotted to the 1950s housewife and advocated that women join the workforce to become more fulfilled.

Highlights:

"There seems to be no doubt that Friedan was on to something. The women in America were truly miserable in their 1950s housewifey roles. However, that may well be a difficult concept to get our heads around because it's so contrary to the common depictions of the decade, most of which seem very vintagey and quaint and squeaky clean and June Cleaver-ish. We tend to want to look at the 50s as that moment when America was happy and healthy and wholesome—before the radical 60s bundled us all into the handbasket and launched us on our journey to Hell.... The widespread cultural rejection of traditional femininity in the 60s should show us that the resentment had been building for a while." (63-64)

"Let's say that during the 60s, instead of the sexual revolution that we actually had, there had been another Great Awakening. What impact would repentance have had on the role of women in the culture? If, in her misery and unhappiness, America had fallen to her knees instead of throwing herself into the pursuit of licentiousness, would there have been any resultant change in the way women were viewed? Absolutely there would have been. I would argue that one of the first things that we would have needed to chuck out the window would have been the idealistic, superficial, and incredibly shallow view of homemaking that was flourishing in the 50s." (70-71)

Questions for Discussion and Application:
1. Who was Betty Friedan? What was the "feminine mystique" problem that she described? What was her solution?

2. What are more women doing today because of second-wave feminism? What are women doing less because of feminism?

3. How do both conservatives and progressives misunderstand the larger story of the 20th century? What would true repentance and reformation have looked like in the 1960s?

Study the Word:
Read Nehemiah 8 and 2 Corinthians 2:8-11. How did the people repent? Why did Ezra and Nehemiah tell the people to rejoice, despite their sins? What separates godly sorrow from despairing sorrow?

6
WOMEN DISAPPOINTED

Summary:
Housewives of the 1950s no longer had a challenging vocation due to America's sudden wealth.

Highlights:
"For a woman of that generation, being a homemaker was an enormous job. Massive. Getting your family through the winter was a big deal. Gardening, for a woman like her, wasn't just a

hobby, it was crucially important. Those women had to work like crazy if they wanted to feed and clothe their families. Not only was the work incredibly difficult, it took skill, perseverance, and creativity. It also included the possibility of a huge amount of satisfaction in a job well done or devastating consequences of failure. It involved risk. These women were playing high-stakes poker, and they had to get good at it." (75-76)

"One understands why, by the late 50s, the women felt like the work was demeaning—but I can't imagine Great-Grandma Hawkins feeling like her work was demeaning. Difficult, yes, but demeaning? She was working shoulder to shoulder with her husband, carving out a life for themselves and their children from the still-untamed wilderness in the new state of Idaho.... But a woman in the 50s who was just supposed to stay at home and keep her hair nice and play bridge and put the TV dinner in the oven at the right time and remember to be charming when her husband rolled in the door from doing big important stuff out in the world—'demeaning' is just about right." (77-78)

Questions for Discussion and Application:
1. What did a housewife have to do before the 1950s? How were both the man and woman necessary for the running of a farm? How did this give women a sense of purpose and competence and value?

2. What did the wealth of the 1950s do for women? What did women spend most of their time doing? How did this contribute to their unhappiness?

3. What bad seeds were being planted in many "ideal" 1950s families? How are we harvesting the fruit of these bad seeds now?

Study the Word:
Read Deuteronomy 8. What does Moses warn the people of Israel may happen if God blesses them? What would wealth tempt the people of Israel to think about themselves? How does this fit our current cultural situation?

7

EXCUSING BOREDOM

Summary:
1950s housewives were discontent, and so they turned to feminism.

Highlights:
"Christ did not tell us that when someone takes our coat we should loudly demand its immediate return. He did not urge us to throw elbows when someone tries to sit in the most important seat. When we are reviled, He did not tell us

to make sandwich boards and picket. When we are struck, we are not told to strike back harder. When Paul was wrongly imprisoned, he didn't commence organizing a prison riot or, for that matter, go on a hunger strike. And yet, aggressively demanding that everyone give women what is owed to us has been the entire campaign strategy of the feminist movement from Day One." (84-85)

"The feminist cause has been advanced for the last two centuries in large part through the diligent efforts of sincere but muddle-headed Christians who never bothered to ask how and why, and jumped on board anyway—and now they're confused by all the consequences they never saw coming. They've been diligently playing basketball and never noticed that they were shooting on the wrong hoop—they still can't figure out why the scoreboard doesn't look better." (92-93)

Questions for Discussion and Application:
1. What is the problem with thinking that the 1950s housewives were simply victims? What are some ways people enjoy blaming their current

problems on their circumstances instead of on how they responded to those circumstances?

2. What is the problem with an angry or shrill political voice, whether on the right or on the left? What are some modern examples? What is the problem with screaming for your rights, even if you have a legitimate demand?

Study the Word:
Read Philippians 4. What kind of suffering had Paul been through (cf. 2 Cor. 11)? What had Paul learned to be in every situation? What does Paul say we should do when we are anxious?

8

SUBDUE

Summary:
Women are made to work!

Highlights:
"What do we know about God? Is He interested in creatures that are dull, underappreciated, and underutilized? Oh for pity's sakes. He's the God who created the tiger. The eagle. The sun. The palm tree. Why on earth, when He got to mankind, would He suddenly decide that He

wanted to top it all off with a creature that's not allowed to live up to its full potential and has to sputter along at 10 percent output, never allowed to get out of first gear? I think we're safe on that front. I'm pretty sure that we'll find that what God has created us for is far more breathtaking, crazy, scary, and glorious than we have wanted to assume, and I don't think any of us, if we throw ourselves into the roles that He sets for us, will find ourselves bored." (99-100)

"Women were created by God to run. To charge at things. To work like crazy. I think this is actually why women can be incredibly successful in the corporate world... If a woman successfully replaces a family with a career in her personal priorities, she is capable of laying herself down for it to an almost absurd degree. That won't necessarily make her happy, mind you. If the racehorse figures out how to run in a circle in the backyard over and over and over all day, it's showing you that it's capable of running—but surely everyone can see that the setting is all wrong. The horse is blowing off steam, not truly doing what it loves and what it was made to do. It's actually capable of so, so much more if it were given the scope." (104)

Questions for Discussion and Application:
1. Why is it important that work was not the result of the fall? How does the Dominion Mandate apply to women?

2. What is wrong with the helplessness of the Victorian stereotype? Why are women frustrated when they spend their lives working for corporations and not for their families?

Study the Word:
Read Genesis 1-2. What were Adam's two tasks? How does Eve help Adam with each of these tasks? Do we usually think of women as helping men with their work?

9

FILL

Summary:
A woman is made to fill the earth with more people.

Highlights:
"The desire to get out into the workplace was never the whole package—and the fact that feminists talk about sex all the time is no accident. What is the biggest hindrance to a career? Being tied down by children. And unless women

are willing to sacrifice their sexuality in the pursuit of their career and become nuns in devout service to the corporation, they have to deal with the fact that they will get pregnant....We live in a society which despises fruitfulness, tolerating it only when it is a sort of self-conscious decision—a baby added on as a little garnish on top of a successful career like the small flourish of kale on the side of your dinner plate. Not really necessary, just decorative, and definitely not the point of the meal." (109)

Questions for Discussion and Application:
1. To state a thought crime: Why is a woman better suited to have a baby than a man? How are women better suited to the home than to the workplace?

2. How does a corporate career interfere with a woman having a family? How is it advantageous to corporations that women are encouraged to join the workforce?

Study the Word:
Read 1 Timothy 5:1-16. What does Paul warn that widows should do if they are young? What does he say women should be doing? How is a woman's vocation tied to her household?

10

HELP

Summary:
A woman is made to help her man.

Highlights:
"The real trouble comes in when we read 'helper' and mentally say, 'inferior.' Once you've done that you're on the wrong path completely. One sees how it happens, of course. 'Helper' implies that someone else is in charge, and the helper is in a secondary role. And having one person chosen

to be the 'head' (1 Cor. 11:3) makes us assume that those responsible for placing that person in charge must think that person is inherently better at certain things—that must be why they were chosen for the task. And if they are 'better' at certain things that implies that the one who wasn't chosen is 'worse.' And 'worse' obviously implies 'inferior.' We run through those steps so quickly we don't even see ourselves doing it— we say 'helper' and think 'inferior' without even noticing the intervening steps." (112-113)

Questions for Discussion and Application:

1. Who does Paul say woman was made for? What should women helping men look like?

2. What is happening when we assume that "helper" means "inferior"? Why is this such a successful lie?

3. What are some ways that feminism, ironically, demands that women cultivate masculine strengths (i.e., physical competitiveness, aggressive leadership, argumentative-ness, etc.)? How does feminism devalue feminine strengths (i.e., tenderness, emotional supportiveness, conflict-averseness)?

Study the Word:
Read Genesis 18:1-15, 21:1-13, and 1 Peter 3:1-6. How does Sarah support Abraham? What does Peter praise her for? How does Sarah serve as a counselor to Abraham? Does God approve of Sarah's advice?

11

GLORIFY

Summary:
A woman is made to glorify.

Highlights:
"Because we women are the glory, it makes sense that we tend to be preoccupied with glorifying. We do this innately and without even having to think about it, in the same way that our bodies can create another human inside of us without us having to stop and read a

manual about how to do it. God created us for this purpose, and we beautify and we glorify constantly. Sometimes we do this in obedient ways, sometimes in rebellious ways; sometimes we revolt against our innate desire to do this at all, but this is a deeply ingrained trait that God has built into womankind, and it just can't be completely smothered. We do it in small things like when we take an unholy looking bachelor pad and turn it into a beautiful home, or when we take a paycheck and turn it into a hot meal on the table that looks and smells and tastes amazing. Women are built to enflesh. To translate." (121-122)

Questions for Discussion and Application:
1. What does 1 Corinthians 11 say woman is the glory of? Is a woman inferior if she is the glory of man, as man is the glory of God?

2. How is submission connected to glory? What is genuine submission? What is wrong with saying all women submit to all men?

Study the Word:
Read Philippians 2:1-15. How did Jesus not grasp after greatness, despite the fact that He was

equal with God? How can we share this same mind of Christ? What are some applications Paul gives in verses 12-15?

12

HOME

Summary:
A woman's first priority is to subdue, fill, help, and glorify in her home.

Highlights:
"Too often we just accept the premise that a homemaker drives carpool, gets the casserole in the oven, and organizes the closets. Once those things are done, we feel like we have ticked all the boxes and now our time is our own. It's all

too easy for us to work in order that we may have leisure, rather than working because we're convinced that we're building something phenomenal—and that mindset makes absolutely all the difference in the world. It is the difference between the employee and the boss, the hired help and the entrepreneur, the servant and the free man." (141)

"Women are born translators. We take principles, abstract ideas, and then put flesh on them. This is just as much a single woman's gift as it is a married woman's—it's just that the application will look different. The single woman should look at the principles—and then figure out how to enflesh them in her particular situation." (143)

Questions for Discussion and Application:

1. Why is it important to submit to God's word with joy instead of apologizing for it?

2. Why do you think that Bekah says that a woman's place is *not* in the home, but instead that her *priority* is in the home? How does Proverbs 31 show us this?

3. How did the industrial revolution change the home? What are some ways you could make your home a center of work again? What are some areas you would be interested in pursuing excellence in how you run the home?

Study the Word:
Read Ruth 1-4. What great kindnesses does Ruth show to Naomi? How is Ruth a great example of loyalty? What does she do before she meets Boaz that shows she is the ideal wife?

13

SUBDUING MADE REAL

Summary:
Excelling in the home requires imagination and intellect.

Highlights:
"What are the things that a woman at home spends time on? One obvious place is food. Everyone's hungry, and it's usually mom's job to make that problem go away. There are two

ways of going about this. The first is to feel bugged at everyone for being hungry again, darn it. So you feed them in a way that resolves the problem with the least amount of disruption to yourself.... The second way to approach the problem of feeding everyone is to say to yourself, 'This is a task that I have to do every single day—I had better figure out how to get good at it.' So you start thinking through the significance of the task. You start asking questions like, 'Why has God made us get hungry and have this need to eat every day? What does He want us to learn? How can I use this to teach my kids about God's goodness, His generosity, His grace, His overwhelming kindness, and use it to embody grace to my husband, my children, and my guests?'" (153-155)

"Could Christian women actually pursue excellence in this field in a way that would change our cultural expectations? Not by awkwardly trying to copy women of the past (please no) but rather by trying to learn from them. By trying to take some of the effort and the craft and the appreciation of quality that went into fashion in earlier days and bring that across in a way that actually resonates now?" (158)

Questions for Discussion and Application:
1. What is the problem with seeing the home as a boring place? What is the problem with just doing the bare minimum of work?

2. Do you love food? What are little non-essential things that you already do to make food nicer?

3. How could Christian women pursue excellence in clothing? Why is it important that homemakers be dressed well?

4. Why is the home so important? What are some specific areas of the home that you have always been interested in and wished you could do more with? What are some tiny things that you can do to get into them?

Study the Word:
Read Matthew 25. What is the larger context of the parable of the talents about? How does the wicked servant excuse his fear? What does the master praise the good servants for getting right? Do we often turn away from responsibility because it is faithfulness over little?

14

FILLING MADE REAL

Summary:

A woman has a powerful ability to take the truths of the gospel and give them real-world beauty.

Highlights:

"If theology is a river, women dig the canals that bring the water into every part of the garden. Righteous women preach the truth, but in parable, metaphor, incarnate poetry. What the pastors explain with words, women sing with hot food, with wine, with welcoming homes, with love and joy that spills out into everything they touch and that draws people irresistibly to the truth that is being embodied." (173)

"Our job as women—and it's a phenomenal responsibility—is to enflesh the weighty truths of our faith. If our role is to make truth *taste*, to make holiness *beautiful*, then what does that look like in the details? As a random example of this, take Christmas.... We take one of the most difficult theological truths—the Incarnation—and attempt to show that truth through our celebrations. The men can talk about the Incarnation, church fathers can write important treatises about it, pastors can preach about it, theologians can parse and define it ... but we women are the ones who make it taste like something. We make it smell good. How crazy is that?" (175)

Questions for Discussion and Application:
1. What is the problem with seeing jobs such as preaching or being a leader as the only important ones? How does this imply that masculine strengths are better or more important than feminine ones?

2. What is the difference between how men bring about change and how women bring about change? How do women take abstract things and put flesh on them?

3. Why is it false to say that, since women can never teach theology, they can never learn theology? Why is education so important for women? How does it help them with home-making?

Study the Word:
Read Esther 5 and 7. How does Esther win the king over? How do her virtues differ from a man's virtues?

15

HELPING MADE REAL

Summary:
A woman should pay close attention to helping *her* people—and that means she must study and love them.

Highlights:
"What does your husband love? How does he like to spend his time? How does he want his children raised? Figure it out, and then run with that. Make it happen, and make it happen in a

way that takes his breath away—a way that he could never have achieved alone. And don't look at what the other women are doing unless you're going to translate it before incorporating the idea—don't try to be the helper to a husband you don't have. That would just be trying to be the knife when what's required is a can opener." (188)

"You take the truth of the gospel and you translate it into beautiful and compelling and incarnate life which preaches the goodness of God to everyone surrounding you. Every Christian woman is called to this, regardless of her particular station in life." (190)

Questions for Discussion and Application:
1. What does Bekah mean when she says that women should "translate" their men's interests and desires? How is it helpful to be attentive to your particular husband's tastes?

2. What are some ways single women can be people-oriented even though they are not married? How can Christian families help include single women in their lives?

Study the Word:
Read Titus 2:3-5. What are older women to teach younger women? What temptations are women supposed to resist and what duties are they supposed to perform?

16

GLORIFYING MADE REAL

Summary:
A submissive woman is glorious, no matter what the world says.

Highlights:
"Be the glory of your husband. Be the concentrated, intoxicating, incarnate poetry that tells the story of death and resurrection, and then throw yourself into the task of glorifying. Be

fruitful. Build your house. Work hard. Be ambitious. Be productive. Learn more. Run harder. Take the gifts God has given you, the desires He has given you, the constraints that he has given you, and then figure out how to weave those into something glorious, something compelling, a beautiful aroma that can't be contained and that beckons a broken world to come and taste, to see that the Lord is good." (194-195)

Questions for Discussion and Application:
1. How is a submissive and sacrificial woman glorious? Why does glory always include a mess (including some in our homes)?

2. How can women be the glory of their husband? Why is this not degrading to a woman?

Study the Word:
Read 2 Corinthians 4. How does Paul describe himself? How is his inner man growing even while his body is perishing? What glory are we supposed to look forward to?

CONCLUSION: RESTORING THE PATHS

Summary:
Women destroyed our culture; women can rebuild it.

Highlights:
"American mothers have outdone Stalin for body count, outstripped Hitler, run circles around Pol Pot. American mothers have waged a war on motherhood itself, and this is a war with real casualties, with real blood, and with fifty-eight million unmarked graves in our

nation's landfills. And Adam called his wife's name Eve, because she was the mother of all living—and we Americans have insisted on hacking away the fertility of Eve so that the name Eve itself might become meaningless. 'We might still be stuck with bodies that get pregnant—but at least you can't make us be the mothers of the living . . . we'll be the mothers of the dead, thank you very much.'" (199)

"We need to rebuild a nation. God has called us to take dominion over an entire planet, and we should start with the mess that is right in front of us. That's a huge job, and so we need to not be satisfied with small. If our biggest goals and dreams are to have a lot of Instagram followers, we'll have a lot to answer for on Judgment Day. But although we need to not be satisfied with small, we also need to not despise the small . . . because in the logic of the gospel it is the small things that turn out to be the greatest (Zech. 4:10). The two mites turn out to be the biggest gift. The glass of cold water to a child turns out to be hugely significant. So don't be satisfied with small, but don't despise the small things that are actually huge things. Learn to tell the difference. What you do in your living room with three little toddlers when no one else is there to see you actually has huge implications." (203)

Questions for Discussion and Application:
1. Why do you think women are often, tragically, at the forefront of the abortion industry? Why are women often the most active in social media political campaigns or in volunteering for a cause? In what ways have men abdicated the world to women?

2. How can women rebuild our country? How would the world look if all women were "quite and peaceable" on social media? How would their families change if they had this spirit?

Study the Word:
Read Ephesians 5-6. What duties does Paul point people to? What metaphor does Paul use to describe what the Christian life actually is like? Who are we fighting?